Scroll Saw Farm Puzzles

By Tony and June Burns

Fox Chapel Publishing Co. Inc.

1970 Broad Street • East Petersburg, PA 17520 • www.foxchapelpublishing.com

Dedication
We dedicate this book to the American Farmer.

Acknowledgments
We wish to thank the following individuals who have helped to make this book possible:
Our children, Jeremy, Emily, Anne and Holly for their inspiration
Our parents for their continued support
Ernesto C. Mellon of the Eclipse Scroll Saw Company
Alan Giagnocavo of Fox Chapel Publishing Co, Inc.
Ayleen Stellhorn of Fox Chapel Publishing Co, Inc.

Publisher:	Alan Giagnocavo
Editor:	Ayleen Stellhorn
Layout and Design:	Alan Davis
Interior Photography :	June Burns and Tony Burns
Cover and Gallery Photography:	Tim Mize

ISBN # 1–56523–138–4

To order your copy of this book,
please send check or money order
for the cover price plus $3.00 shipping to:
Fox Books
1970 Broad Street
East Petersburg, PA 17520

Or visit us on the web at
www.foxchapelpublishing.com

Manufactured in Korea
10 9 8 7 6 5 4 3 2 1

Because scrolling wood and other materials inherently includes the risk of injury and damage, this book cannot guarantee that creating the projects in this book is safe for everyone. For this reason, this book is sold without warranties or guarantees of any kind, express or implied, and the publisher and authors disclaim any liability for any injuries, losses or damages caused in any way by the content of this book or the reader's use of the tools needed to complete the projects presented here. The publisher and the authors urge all scrollers to thoroughly review each project and to understand the use of all tools involved before beginning any project.

Table of Contents

About the Authors

We tapped into the roots of our childhoods for ideas on this, our second book. The fact that both of us grew up in western New York, surrounded by beautiful countryside, became a great inspiration for the designs in this book. We enjoy the outdoors and nature. June loves to "dig in the dirt" and grow things. Tony loves animals and loves a nice long walk in the woods with Benny, his dog. Our children are nature nuts, too. They bring all sorts of critters home so they can "watch them grow," as they so sweetly put it. June has to carefully check pockets before any clothing goes into the washer.

We hope you enjoy this book as much as we enjoyed creating the designs for you.

Happy Scrolling!
Tony and June Burns

Tony and June welcome your comments and questions, as well as your suggestions for future works. Please include a self-addressed, stamped envelope for a response.

Tony and June Burns
4744 Berry Road
Fredonia, NY 14063

Introduction

As a small boy back in the 1960s, I can remember many a hot summer's day when my parents would take my two brothers and me to visit my Great Uncle's farm in Olean, New York. My Grandmother was one of twelve children who grew up on a farm. She was one of the nicest people that God had ever put on this earth, and it's more than likely because she was no stranger to hard work and had a loving heart. I can remember fondly chasing the chickens and having "Uncle Ed" tell me that if I could catch one, I could have it. My brothers and I finally did corner an old hen and proudly carried it to him. I can remember watching him laugh louder than I've ever heard anyone laugh. Of course, you could probably guess that my Mom sternly said, "No." I had to let the old hen go. I remember those days fondly.

Chautaqua, New York, is where June and I live with our four children. This land is loaded with numerous farms and hundreds of acres of grapes. It's not uncommon to find a tractor driving down the middle of the road. With all of this in mind, we dedicate this book to the American Farmer, for whom we have a great love and to whom we can never give enough thanks.

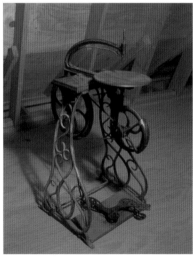

A sampling of antique saws.

Gallery

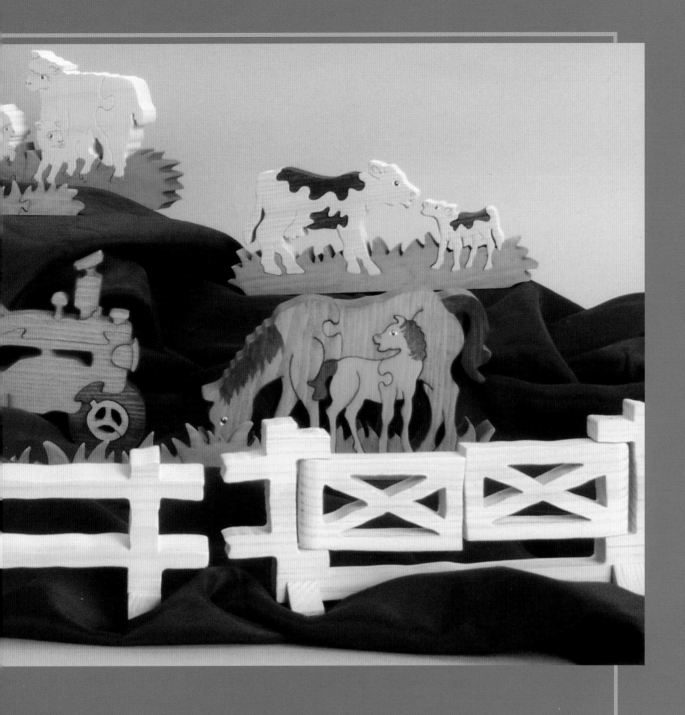

Getting Started

Selecting wood

We prefer to use silver maple, basswood and pine. These woods are readily available in our area and are relatively easy for beginners to cut. Denser woods and plywood are stronger but are harder to cut. We have had fairly good success with 19mm solid core Baltic or Finnish Birch.

Learning about the density of each particular type of wood is important. This will help you to determine how strong a piece of wood is for a particular purpose. It also helps you to assess the ease of cutting and the type of blade to use.

We have a great love for oak and butternut, the latter being easier to cut. These harder woods, including Baltic and Finnish Birch, tend to dull blades faster, but they add fun and challenges to a great project. Your local supplier may have these or other varieties from which to choose.

When purchasing wood for puzzles, we suggest that you buy the best grade of wood that you can afford. Look for wood with a straight grain and few defects. Also avoid lumber which appears damp or heavier than usual. The following are the most common defects in wood that affect puzzle making.

Warping: Avoid any wood that is obviously warped or twisted.

Cracks: Cracks occur in the end grain and along the grain of many boards. They are hard to see. A bright light will help to make them visible.

If a board has cracks along the grain, known as checking, it probably has more and is worthless. Even if you think you can squeeze your pattern on after the crack, there is most likely another crack there that goes unnoticed. When you see checking, there is a good chance more wood of the same lot has the same effect. The wood was probably cut from the same tree or improperly dried.

Knots: You can work around most knots, but many times they are visible on only one side of the board. Check both sides before laying out a pattern.

Preparing to cut

Lubricate the table: I have found that lubricating the table with paste wax helps to reduce friction and allows your project to move freely on the saw table. This especially helps when your saw table is cast iron. The lubricant helps to keep the table from rusting, which can inhibit your project's movement. (Heavily coat the table if it's going to sit for an extended amount of time between uses.)

Square the blade: It is a good idea to occasionally check the "squareness" of your cut. To do so, use a small 2-inch engineer's square. Adjust the table to 90 degrees. This can be done on a weekly basis or as needed.

Check the blade thickness: A micrometer is another good investment. Being able to verify the thickness and the width of a blade helps to troubleshoot problems. It is also a good way to verify a blade size in the event the blades get mixed up.

Light the area: Good lighting is necessary when cutting. Incandescent light is easier on the eyes than fluorescent. If your saw is not sold with a light, most manufacturers sell a light kit or a magnifying lens separately.

Buy an anti-vibration mat: I have found that placing one under the saw reduces vibration and operator fatigue.

Use safety gear: Three areas of safety concern are ears, eyes and respiration. A quality set of comfortable hearing protectors or ear plugs are a must if you cut for any extended period of time. For proper eye protection, quality safety glasses with side shields are necessary. If you wear tempered prescription glasses you can purchase eye shields for them.

As avid scrollers we are concerned with the quality of the air we breathe when we operate machinery. A good quality respirator is necessary to trap the fine dust and particles in the air. In addition to this, we have a permanent air filtration system mounted on the ceiling and a portable unit on wheels.

About scroll saw blades

Fret saw blades (scroll saw blades) are typically made from high carbon steel that is heated, forged and drawn over many miles of rollers. This makes the steel thinner and thinner until it becomes wires of the desired thickness. The wires are then flattened. If you look closely, you will notice a slight curvature on the back of most blades. This is an indication that the blades started out as wires. After the steel is flattened, the particular teeth style and size are ground into the steel.

Blades can also be made by a punch or through a shearing action. They are not typically made this way today, however, because these blades are not as sharp or as uniform as ground blades. We have a small collection of many of these older blades that are hand made and came off treadle machines used during the late 1800s to early 1900s.

Choosing a blade

Blades are the heart and soul of a scroll saw. The finest scroll saw will not work to its full potential if you are using the wrong blade.

For fine cutting ³⁄₄-inch (19mm) or 1-inch wood, we suggest that you start with a #3 or a #5 blade. These blades will give you better detail and smoother cuts. There is no rule that says you must

use a #3 or a #5 blade. Keep in mind though that a smaller blade, such as #0 or #2, will take longer to cut and may burn the wood from the extra friction. The larger blades, #9 and #12, are easier to use when you are cutting straight lines or larger radiuses, but they are not the best choice for detail. These larger blades do not leave as fine of an edge on the wood and may require more sanding than a finer blade. Larger blades also make the puzzles looser, which may or may not be desirable.

Blade sizes may vary from one manufacturer to another. For example, what one manufacturer calls a #2 blade may be extremely close to another company's #3 blade. TPI (teeth per inch) may also be measured differently from one manufacturer to the next. One company may measure teeth from tip to tip; another may measure from gullet to gullet. This can change the teeth count by half of a tooth to a whole tooth.

It is also important to take care of your blades. When blades are stored for long periods of time they tend to rust. We recommend spraying them with a light coat of oil or with WD40 to prevent rusting. We know this trick works first-hand because we use it frequently: we buy all of our blades for the year at the same time.

One of the most common questions we get is: "What is the best blade for my saw?" This question is next to impossible to answer. Each scroll saw handles the same blade differently, and this answer is not a simple one. Experimenting with different types and sizes of blades is one of the best investments you can make. It is also the best way to decide which blade works best for you.

Displaying the finished pieces

An ideal way to display your finished puzzles is to perch them on a shelf above a door as we did on the back cover of this book. Use the patterns on page 67 for the brackets and cut a piece of wood large enough to fit your door frame. Make sure to use wood screws or sheet rock screws to secure the shelf to the wall.

Cutting the Barn

To start this project you'll need a ^{3}/4-inch-thick board that is 11^1/2" x 16" and a #3 or #5 blade. The red lines on the pattern (page 58 and 59) are detail lines for painting and are not intended to be cut. Keep the saw table clean and lubricated with paste wax as you scroll.

The pattern and finished example of the barn are on pages 57, 58 and 59.

Make a copy of the pattern by scanning it into a computer, using a photocopier or tracing it onto tracing paper. Lightly spray the back side of the pattern with spray adhesive and adhere the pattern to the wood. The arrows on the pattern indicate grain direction.

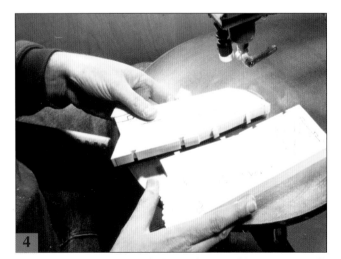

Cut the bottom edge of the barn first. Use your left hand as a guide as you push with your right hand. This will give you a straighter cut.

Continue cutting the outer edge of the barn until the outline is complete. Remove the outer piece of waste wood.

Cut the puzzle in half along the roof line. This will make the puzzle easier to work with.

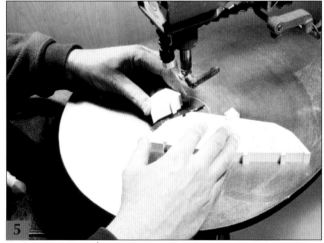

Cut out and remove the silo. Set this piece aside.

How-to

Cut out and remove the cupola.

Cut the roof detail on the roof's front side.

Cut the top half of the roof and separate it from the front and the side of the barn.

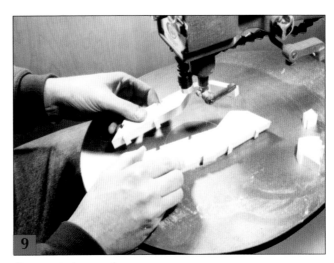

Remove the roof.

Cut the top front of the barn away from the side of the roof.

Cut off the trim board (the narrow strip on the front of the barn).

Remove the trim board.

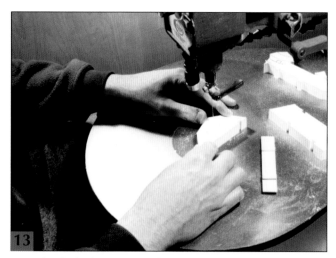

Cut the loft door away from the top of the barn.

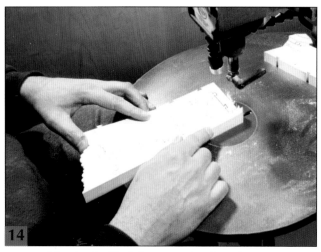

Assemble the half of the puzzle already cut out on a small table next to the scroll saw. Cut the grass and bush away from the barn.

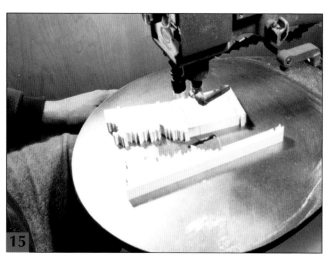

Carefully separate the pieces.

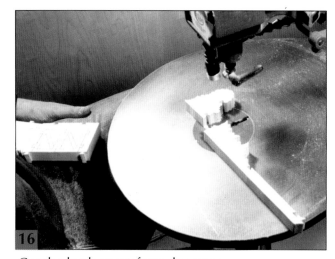

Cut the bush away from the grass.

Cut the front of the barn away from the side.

Separate and remove the side piece.

Cut out the barn doors on the front piece. Only cut the outline, not the center details.

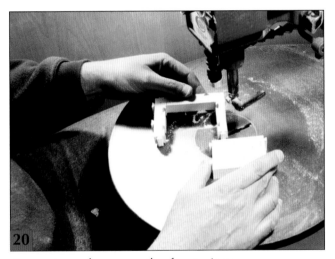

Separate and remove the front piece.

Cut the two front doors apart along the center line.

Remove the pattern from the wood with a heat gun. Be careful; use the gun at its lowest heat setting.

Using a sanding block with 150-grit or 120-grit abrasive paper, sand with the grain to remove any dried adhesive and any small burrs on the wood.

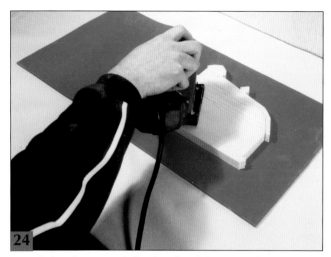

24

Sand the front and the back of the puzzle using 150-grit abrasive paper in a power sander.

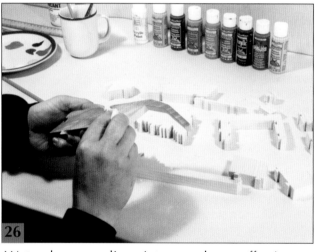

26

Water down acrylic paints to make an effective, yet inexpensive stain. Apply the stain with a brush. Use a rag to wipe away any excess stain.

28

Using a permanent, fine-line marker and straight edge, draw in the line details for doors, the barn and the roof. You may wish to use a pencil first.

25

Hand-sand the edge of each piece with 150-grit sandpaper to remove burrs; then apply a sealer coat to the pieces and allow the sealer to dry. The sealer helps to keep the water-based stains from soaking into the wood too quickly. It also helps to keep the stains from raising the grain of the wood.

27

Allow the pieces to dry completely before proceeding to the next step.

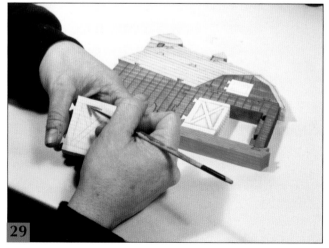

29

Shade the sides of the barn and the details on the door with acrylics.

Cutting the Farmer

We designed this puzzle to have a minimal amount of internal drilling and cutting. For example, the rear wheel only requires one drill hole.

To complete this project you'll need a ³/4-inch-thick board to fit the pattern and a #3 or #5 blade. The pattern and finished example of the farmer are on pages 38 and 39.

Cut only the black lines; the red lines show details to be added with a marker or paint brush.

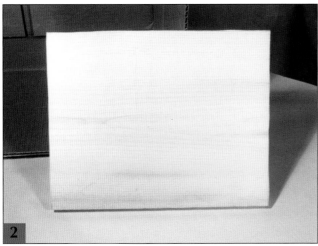

Make a copy of the pattern by scanning it into a computer, using a photocopier or tracing it onto tracing paper.

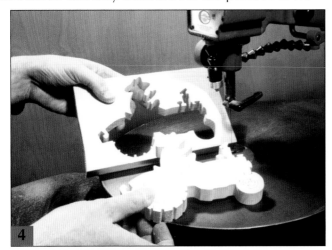

Select a clear, knot-free piece of wood. We used solid wood in the book for its beauty. Solid core Baltic Birch is a lot stronger and more durable—a good idea if the puzzle is intended for a child—but its end grain is very pronounced and may detract from the puzzle's look.

Spray a light coat of adhesive onto the back of the pattern and center the pattern on the wood.

Cut the outline of the tractor and remove the outer piece.

Drill starter holes for the internal cuts on a drill press or use a hand drill fitted with a ¹/8 inch bit. Front wheel (1 hole); rear wheel (1 hole); front engine compartment (1 hole); rear engine compartment (1 hole).

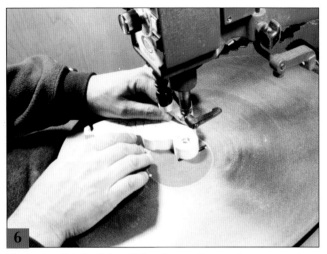

6

Cut out the inside of the front tire and remove the loose pieces.

7 **Cut the remaining parts of the puzzle in the following order.**

Inside rear tire
Front engine compartment
Rear engine compartment
Front wheel
Rear wheel
Rear tire tread detail
Farmer
Farmer's hat
Farmer's beard and head
Edge detail on Farmer's belt and boot
Top of tractor
Waste under steering wheel
Detail for front head light

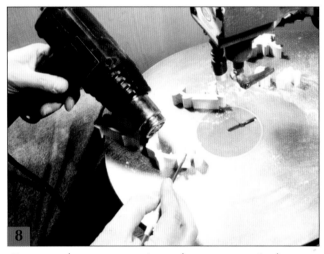

8

Remove the pattern using a heat gun on its lowest setting. I use a metal working scratch awl to remove pattern pieces and to keep my fingers away from the heat.

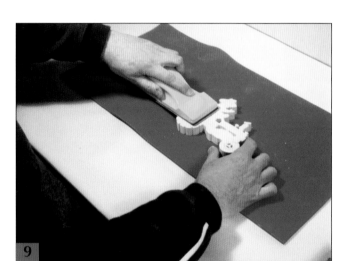

9

Using a 120-grit or 150-grit sanding block, sand with the grain to remove any dried adhesive left from the pattern and to remove any protruding burrs.

10

Sand the front and the back of the work with 150-grit sandpaper in a power palm sander.

11

Hand-sand the edge of each piece to remove any burrs; then apply a clear coat of sanding sealer or finish sealer.

How-to

Stain the pieces with a watered-down acrylic craft paint. A wide variety of colors is available at your local craft store. You may also choose to mix them to get the colors you desire.

Wipe the faces of the pieces to distribute the color evenly. The sealer you applied earlier will help to keep the watered-down acrylics from soaking into the wood and give a more even finish.

Stain and wipe all of the tractor pieces to the colors you desire. Let the pieces dry completely before proceeding with the next step.

Now paint the farmer. Paint the pants, boots and hands on the lower body piece first.

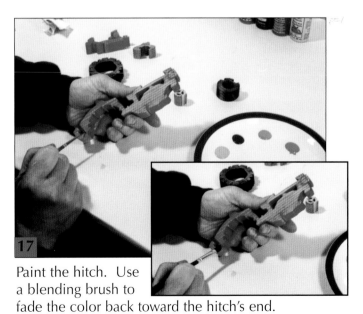

Detail the face. The head and the beard are one puzzle piece; stain it white then paint the face. Use a fine-line permanent marker to draw the farmer's eyes, nose, mouth and ears.

Paint the hitch. Use a blending brush to fade the color back toward the hitch's end.

How-to

Mare and Foal

WOOD GRAIN DIRECTION

© Anthony Burns

Patterns

Cow and Calf

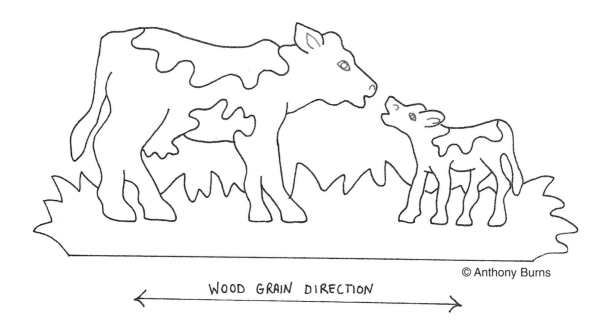

WOOD GRAIN DIRECTION

© Anthony Burns

Patterns

Cow Family

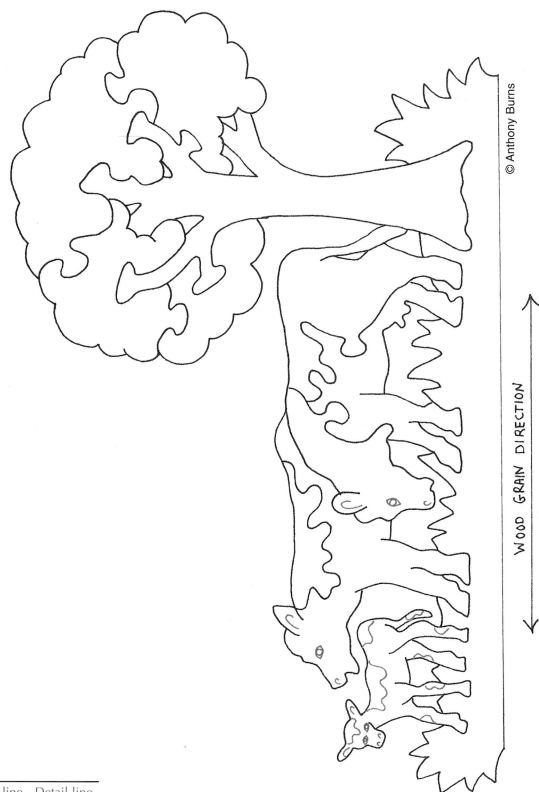

© Anthony Burns

WOOD GRAIN DIRECTION

Red line - Detail line
Black line - Cut line

Sheep and Lambs

© Anthony Burns

WOOD GRAIN DIRECTION

Patterns

Goats and Kid

© Anthony Burns

Red line - Detail line
Black line - Cut line

Hen, Rooster and Chicks

WOOD GRAIN DIRECTION

© Anthony Burns

Patterns

Geese and Goslings

WOOD GRAIN DIRECTION

© Anthony Burns

Patterns

Pig Trio

Red line - Detail line
Black line - Cut line

Patterns

Piglet in Mud

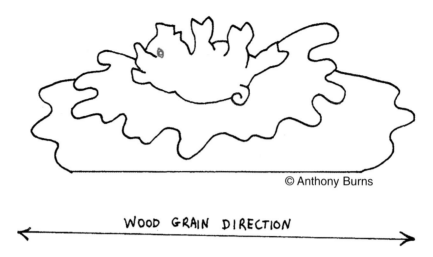

© Anthony Burns

WOOD GRAIN DIRECTION

Chicks and Worm

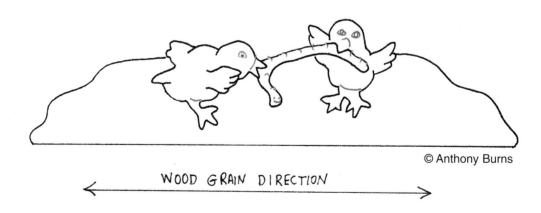

© Anthony Burns

WOOD GRAIN DIRECTION

Patterns

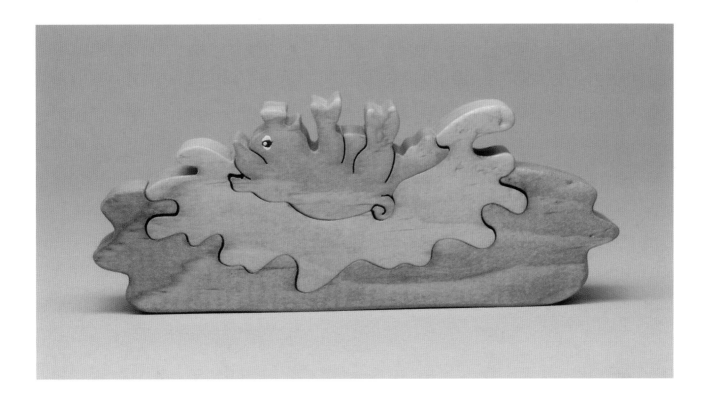

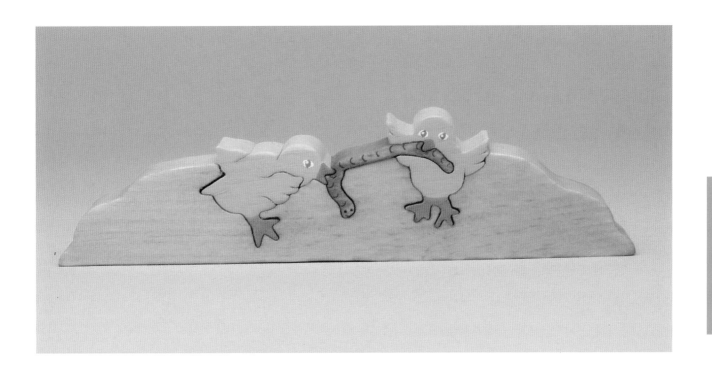

Dog and Dog House

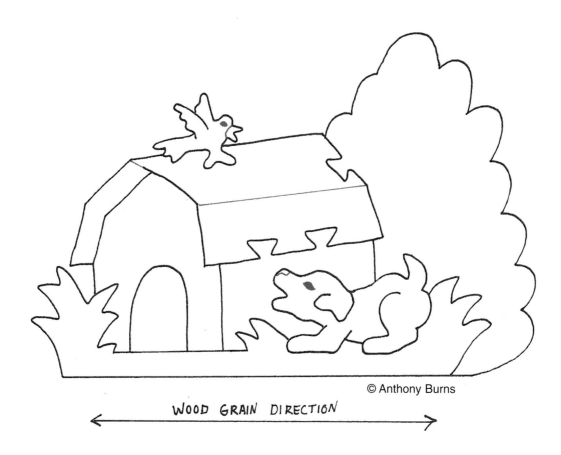

WOOD GRAIN DIRECTION

© Anthony Burns

Patterns

Farmer and Tractor

WOOD GRAIN DIRECTION

© Anthony Burns

Patterns

Hay Wagon

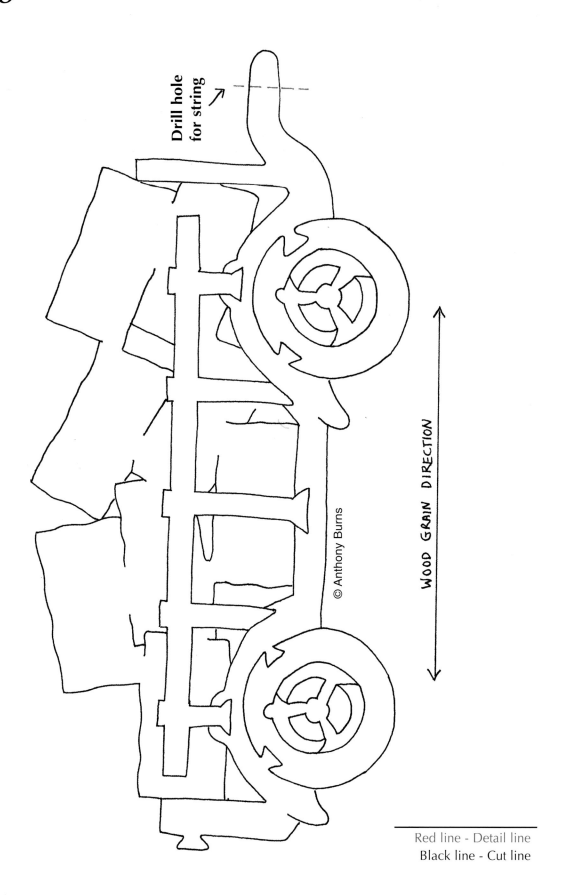

Drill hole for string

WOOD GRAIN DIRECTION

© Anthony Burns

Red line - Detail line
Black line - Cut line

Scarecrow

WOOD GRAIN DIRECTION

© Anthony Burns

Red line - Detail line
Black line - Cut line

Haystack

© Anthony Burns

WOOD GRAIN DIRECTION

Patterns

Pine Trees

© Anthony Burns

WOOD GRAIN DIRECTION

Red line - Detail line

Black line - Cut line

Wishing Well

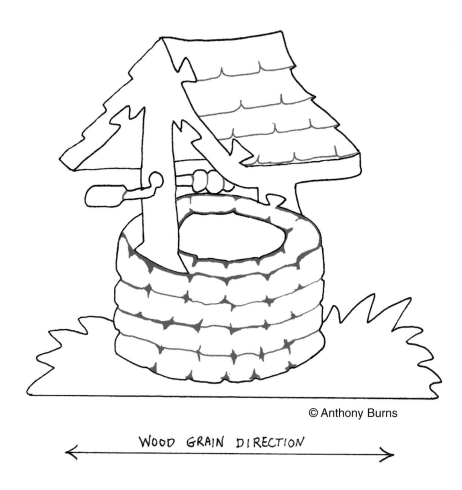

© Anthony Burns

WOOD GRAIN DIRECTION

Outhouse

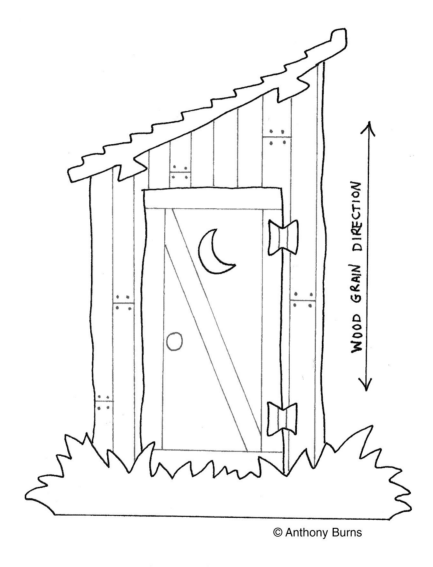

WOOD GRAIN DIRECTION

© Anthony Burns

Red line - Detail line
Black line - Cut line

Pick-Up Truck

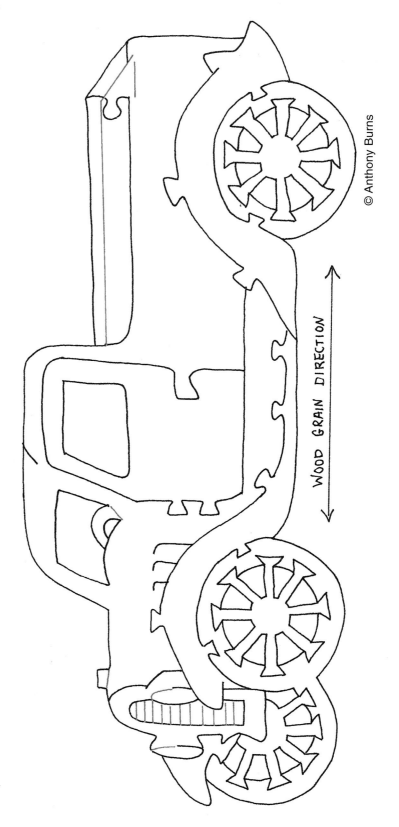

WOOD GRAIN DIRECTION

© Anthony Burns

Patterns

Farm House

© Anthony Burns

Red line - Detail line
Black line - Cut line

N DIRECTION

Patterns

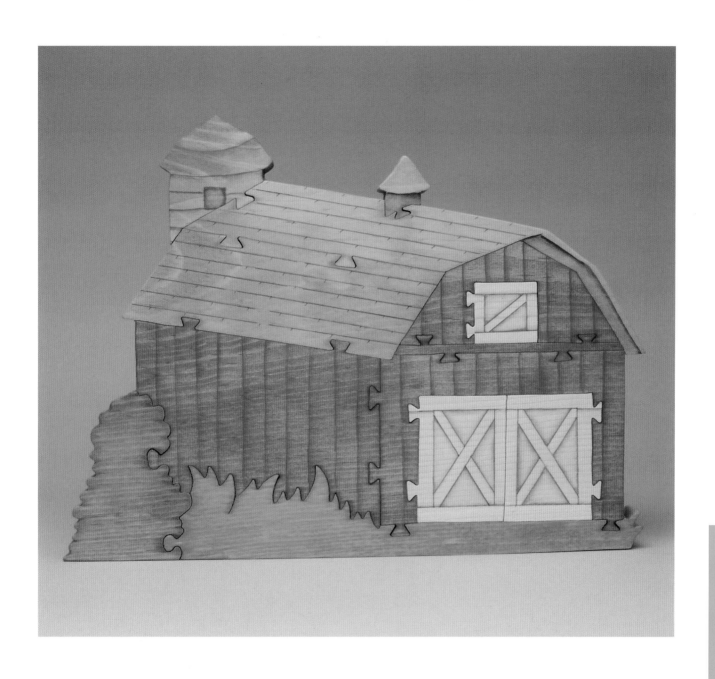

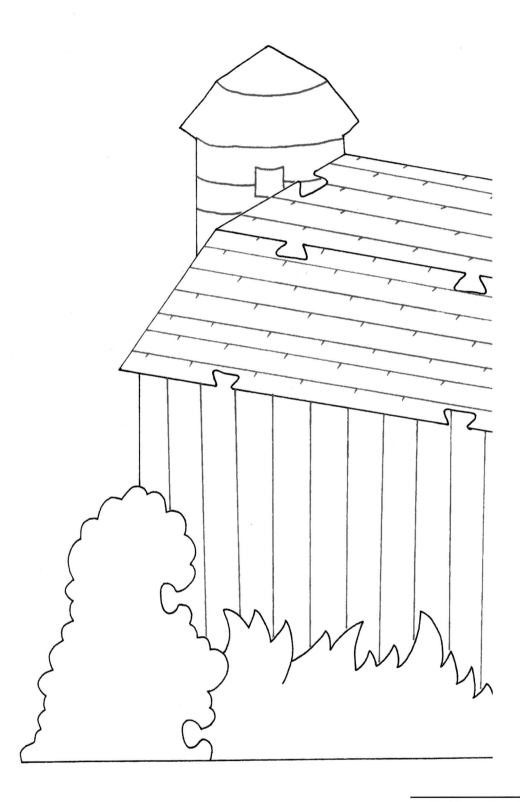

Red line - Detail line
Black line - Cut line

WOOD GRAIN DIRECTION

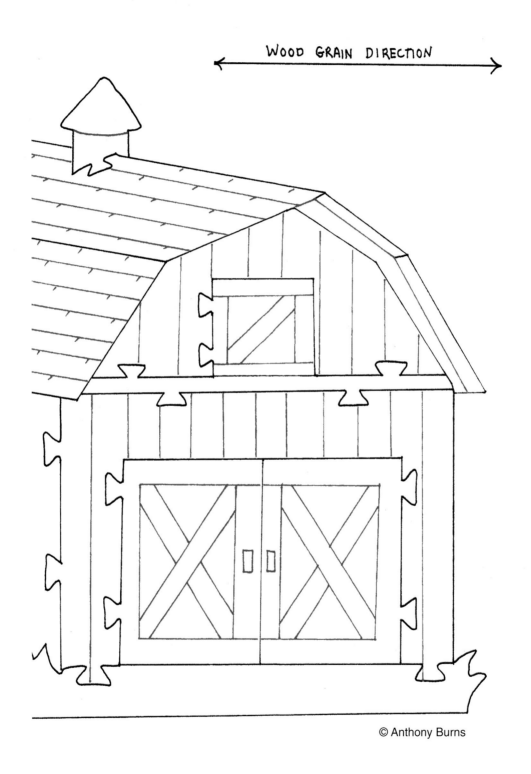

Scroll Saw Farm Puzzles

Chicken House

Red line - Detail line
Black line - Cut line

Patterns

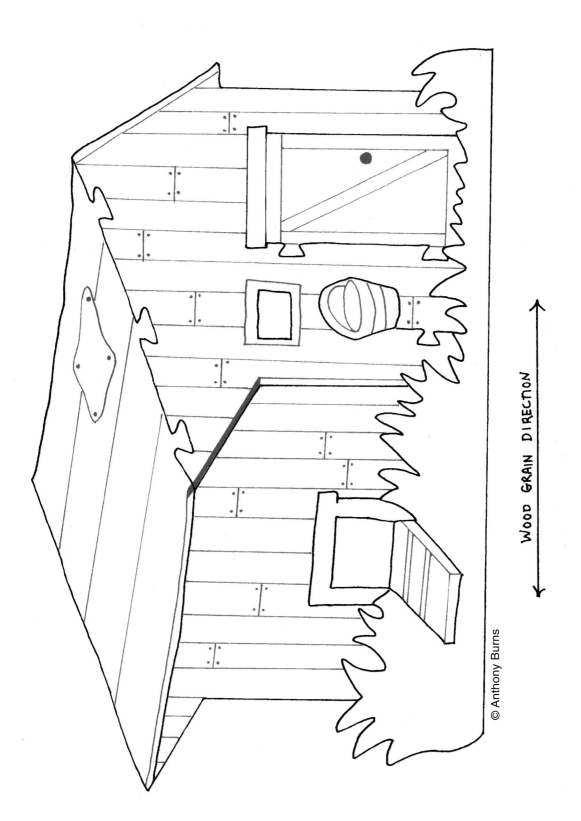

WOOD GRAIN DIRECTION

© Anthony Burns

Grass

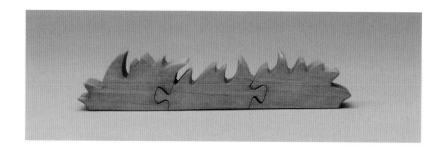

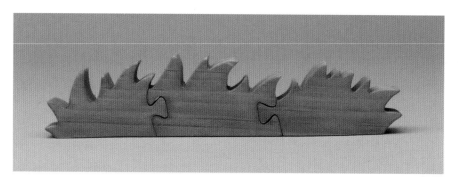

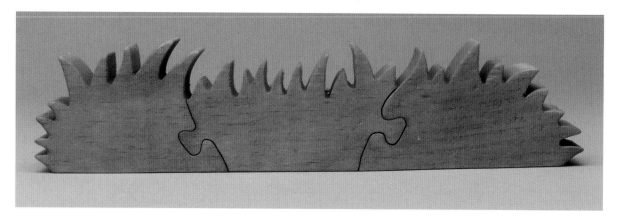

Red line - Detail line
Black line - Cut line

Patterns

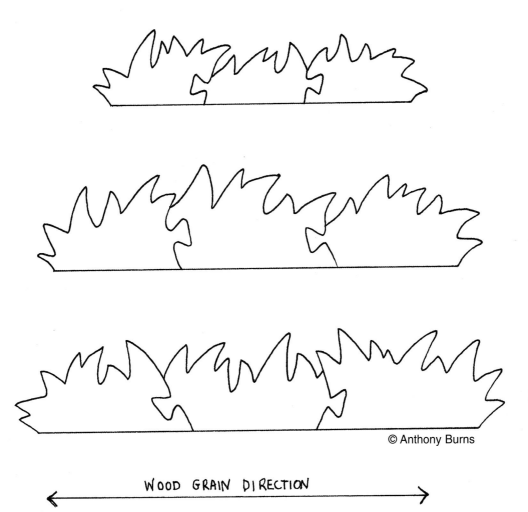

© Anthony Burns

WOOD GRAIN DIRECTION

Patterns

Single Gate

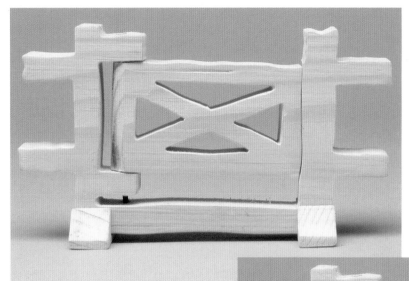

Round the edges on the inside of the gate door so the gate can swing.

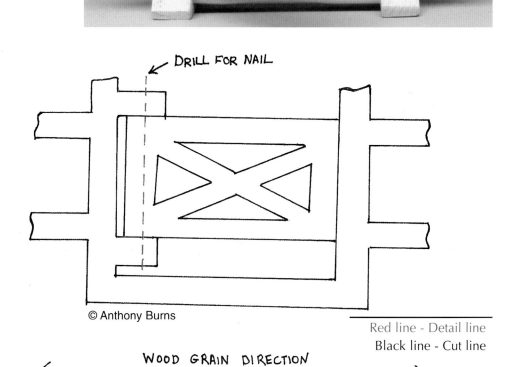

← DRILL FOR NAIL

© Anthony Burns

Red line - Detail line
Black line - Cut line

WOOD GRAIN DIRECTION

Double Gate

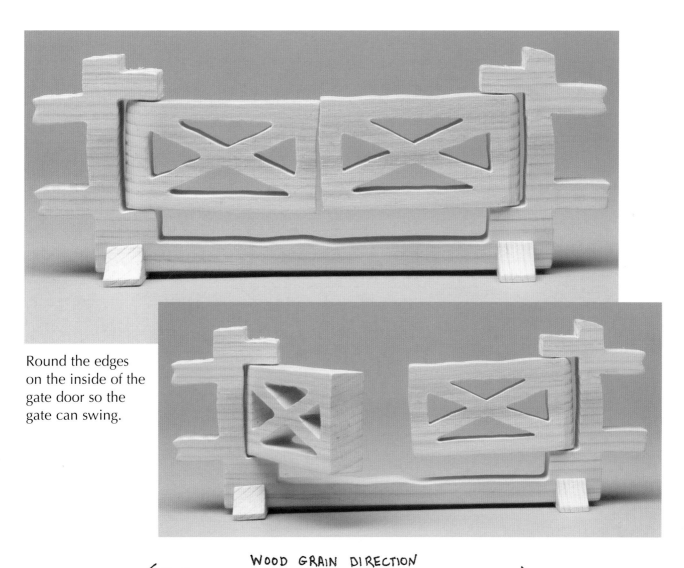

Round the edges on the inside of the gate door so the gate can swing.

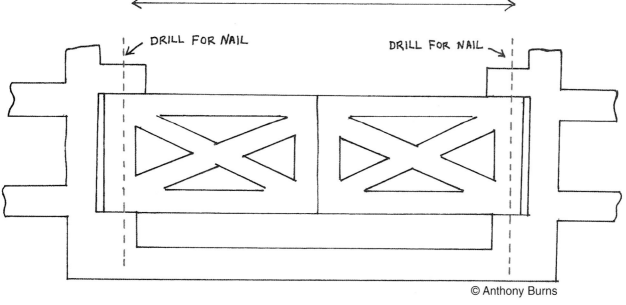

WOOD GRAIN DIRECTION

DRILL FOR NAIL

DRILL FOR NAIL

© Anthony Burns

Patterns

Fence

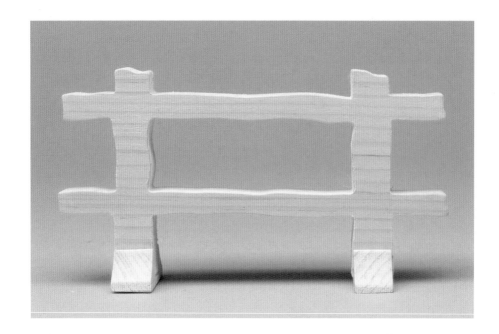

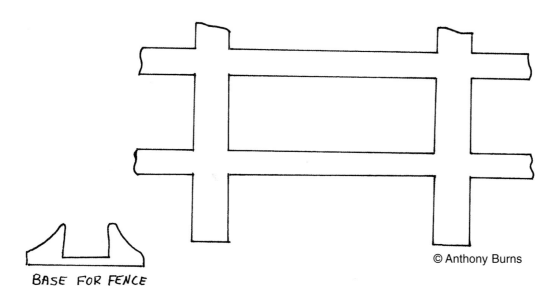

© Anthony Burns

BASE FOR FENCE

Red line - Detail line
Black line - Cut line

Rooster Shelf

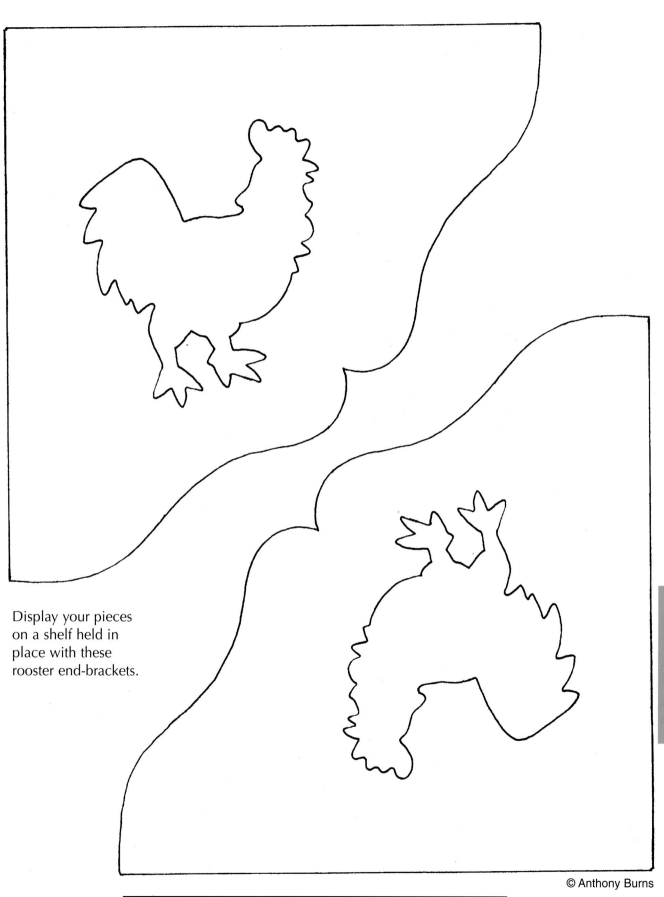

Display your pieces on a shelf held in place with these rooster end-brackets.

© Anthony Burns

More Great Project Books from Fox Chapel Publishing

- **Scroll Saw Art Puzzles by Tony and June Burns:** Everyone loves a good puzzle. Includes step-by-step cutting and painting demonstrations plus patterns for 32 fun puzzle projects including flowers, animals, whales, Noah's ark, and more.
ISBN: 1-56523-116-3, 80 pages, soft cover, $14.95.

- **Dinosaur Puzzles for the Scroll Saw by Judy and Dave Peterson:** Make 30 spectacular dinosaur puzzles - from the terrifying T-Rex to the wading Brontosaurus. Features 30 puzzles and how-to instructions. Puzzles can be made with many pieces for adults or fewer pieces for children.
ISBN: 1-56523-184-8, 72 pages, soft cover, $14.95.

- **Scroll Saw Workbook by John A. Nelson:** The ultimate beginner's scrolling guide! Hone your scroll saw skills to perfection with the 25 skill-building chapters and projects included in this book. Techniques and patterns for wood and non-wood projects!
ISBN: 1-56523-117-1, 88 pages, soft cover, $14.95.

- **Compound Scroll Saw Creations by Diana Thompson:** Cut compound clocks, candlestick holders and characters on your scroll saw. Includes shop-tested patterns, basic instructions and information on wood choices.
ISBN: 1-56523-170-8, 72 pages, soft cover, $14.95.

- **Scroll Saw Toys & Vehicles by Stan Graves:** Make durable wooden toys that will bring smiles to children of any age. Features sturdy, practical designs, ready-to-use patterns for ten vehicles, and full-color photographs of the finished projects.
ISBN: 1-56523-115-5, 42 pages, soft cover, $12.95.

- **Scroll Saw Portraits by Gary Browning:** Learn how to use a computer or photocopier to change any photograph into a pattern for your scroll saw. Includes pattern-making techniques, tips on which photos make good patterns, and 55 portrait patterns.
ISBN: 1-56523-147-3, 96 pages, soft cover, $14.95.

Call 800-457-9112 or visit us on the web at www.foxchapelpublishing.com to order!

Scroll Saw WorkShop
The How-To Magazine for Scrollers

Don't Miss A Single Issue - Subscribe Today!

Each full color issue will contain:

- **Detailed illustrations & diagrams**
- **Ready-to-use patterns**
- **Step-by-step instructions**
- **Crisp, clear photography**
- **Must have tips for beginners**
- **Challenging projects for more advanced scrollers**
- **Interviews with leading scrollers, and more...**

All to help you become the best scroller you can be!

50 EASY WEEKEND SCROLL SAW PROJECTS
By John A. Nelson

FREE with a 2-year paid subscription!
58 Pages, 8.5 x 11 soft cover
$10 value!

Includes:
- *50 simple, useful projects*
- *Easy-to-understand patterns*
- *Practical pieces, including clocks, shelves, plaques and frames*